Victoria Beckham Bio

From Spice to Icon.

By

Clara Berg

Copyright © 2023 by Clara Berg. All rights reserved.

This book, "Victoria Beckham Biography: From Spice to Icon," is the intellectual property of Clara Berg. No part of this publication may be reproduced, distributed, or transmitted in any form or by any means, including photocopying, recording, or other electronic or mechanical methods, without the prior written permission of the author, except for brief quotations embodied in critical reviews and certain other noncommercial uses permitted by copyright law. The author and publisher have made every effort to ensure the accuracy of the information presented but do not assume any liability for errors or omissions.

Disclaimer:

This book, "Victoria Beckham Biography: From Spice to Icon," is a work of non-fiction that aims to provide a comprehensive and informative account of Victoria Beckham' life. While every effort has been made to ensure the accuracy of the information presented, the author, Clara Berg, and the publisher do not warrant or represent that the contents are free from errors, inaccuracies, or omissions.

Readers are encouraged to conduct their own research and verification to supplement the information provided in this book. The author and publisher disclaim any liability for any loss or damage resulting from reliance on the information contained herein. This book is not intended as professional advice, and any decisions or actions based on its content are at the reader's discretion.

All rights reserved. © 2023 Clara Berg.

Table of Contents:

INTRODUCTION — 5
Setting the Stage: The '90s Pop Culture Phenomenon — 5

CHAPTER 1: CHILDHOOD IN ESSEX — 9
Early Years and Family Background — 9

CHAPTER 2: ASPIRING PERFORMER — 13
Victoria's Early Interest in Music and Dance — 13

CHAPTER 3: SPICE GIRLS TAKE THE WORLD BY STORM — 17
The Formation of the Spice Girls and Their Meteoric Rise — 17

CHAPTER 4: THE SPICE GIRLS' GLOBAL DOMINATION — 22
Their Music, Style, and Impact on Pop Culture — 22

CHAPTER 5: POSH SPICE PERSONA — 26
Victoria's Role and Image within the Group — 26

CHAPTER 6: VICTORIA AND DAVID BECKHAM — 30
The Love Story That Captivated the World — 30

CHAPTER 7: BEYOND THE SPICE: VICTORIA'S SOLO MUSIC CAREER — 34

Her Transition to a Solo Artist 34

CHAPTER 8: SPICE GIRLS REUNIONS 37
The Group's Reunions and Their Ongoing Legacy 37

CHAPTER 9: FASHION FORWARD: VICTORIA'S STYLE EVOLUTION 41
Her Influence on the Fashion Industry 41

CHAPTER 10: VICTORIA BECKHAM: THE FASHION DESIGNER 46
Launching Her Eponymous Fashion Brand 46

CHAPTER 11: BUILDING A FASHION EMPIRE 51
The Success and Expansions of Her Fashion Business 51

CHAPTER 12: FAMILY LIFE AND PHILANTHROPY 56
Balancing Motherhood and Her Charitable Work 56

CHAPTER 13: ICONIC MOMENTS AND CONTROVERSIES 60
Key Events That Shaped Her Public Image 60

CHAPTER 14: SPICE GIRLS' LEGACY 64
The Ongoing Impact of the Group 64

CHAPTER 15: VICTORIA'S GLOBAL INFLUENCE 67
Her Cultural Significance and Popularity 67

CHAPTER 16: A DAY IN THE LIFE OF VICTORIA BECKHAM — 71
Insights into Her Daily Routine and Lifestyle — 71

CHAPTER 17: BEHIND THE SCENES: CREATING HER BRAND — 75
The Work and Creativity That Fuels Her Success — 75

CHAPTER 18: VICTORIA'S FUTURE AND ENDURING LEGACY — 79
What Lies Ahead and Her Place in History — 79

CONCLUSION: FROM SPICE TO ICON — 84
Reflecting on Victoria Beckham's Remarkable Journey — 84

Introduction

Setting the Stage: The '90s Pop Culture Phenomenon

The 1990s, a decade of kaleidoscopic change, was unlike any other in the 20th century. It was a time when flannel shirts and neon tracksuits coexisted, and a period of cultural upheaval that set the stage for the global phenomena that would captivate our hearts. And at the heart of this tempestuous era stood none other than Victoria Beckham.

Victoria's journey through the '90s was like a whirlwind romance with the world itself. Born in Harlow, Essex, on April 17, 1974, her early years held no crystal ball to foretell the global icon she would become. She was the youngest of three in a loving family, where her parents, Jacqueline and Anthony, recognized her flair for the performing arts from the get-go.

But as the 1990s dawned, the British music scene was on fire, and a cultural rebellion was sweeping the nation. Bands like the Spice Girls, Oasis, and the Prodigy were the speakers of this youth revolution. Victoria, whose dreams were originally spun around dance, found her destiny in an audition that would change the world. The Spice Girls, a girl group formed through auditions, became an emblem of empowerment, with each member embodying a distinct archetype of female strength. Victoria, poised and chic, slipped naturally into the role of Posh Spice.

In 1996, their debut single, "Wannabe," exploded onto the scene, a bomb of catchy melodies and a lyrical testament to female friendship. It became the anthem of a generation, and the Spice Girls became a cultural tour de force. And at the heart of this whirlwind was Posh Spice, her trademark bob and little black dresses casting a spell over fans globally.

As the Spice Girls' fame soared, so did Victoria Beckham's public persona. Paparazzi lenses followed her every step, from her fashion choices to her blossoming romance with soccer superstar David Beckham. It was an era that saw the birth of modern celebrity culture, where tabloids and fashion magazines became as essential as hit singles.

But beyond the glitz and paparazzi flashes was a woman of remarkable resolve and a vision that transcended the stage. Victoria's journey from the suburbs of Essex to the world stage was marked by hurdles, transformations, and personal growth. Her evolution from Spice Girl to fashion icon bore witness to her adaptability and strength.

This biography is a deep dive into the life of Victoria Beckham, from her early days in Essex to her emergence as a celebrated fashion designer and business mogul. It's a journey that traverses the Spice Girls' meteoric success, her enduring love story with David Beckham, and her profound impact on the world of fashion.

In the pages that follow, we'll unravel the captivating story of Victoria Beckham, exploring her multifaceted life. From her roots in Essex to her prominence in the '90s and beyond, we will uncover the woman behind the fame. This biography is an exploration of a period when a Spice Girl transformed into a global icon, and we're invited to peek behind the curtains to discover the person who created an enduring legacy.

In the upcoming chapters, we'll navigate the intricate and compelling narrative of Victoria Beckham, a journey that commences in her modest beginnings and leads us through the whirlwind of the '90s, a decade that forever changed the landscape of popular culture. From Spice to Icon, this is the chronicle of a woman who not only weathered the storm of fame but harnessed it to build a legacy that continues to inspire millions.

Chapter 1: Childhood in Essex

Early Years and Family Background

As we embark on this exploration of Victoria Beckham's life, we must begin at the very beginning, tracing her footsteps back to the picturesque landscapes of Essex, a county in the East of England. This is where the seeds of her remarkable journey were first sown, amidst the modesty and warmth of her family.

Victoria Caroline Adams, known to the world as Victoria Beckham, came into the world on April 17, 1974. She was the youngest of three children, born to Anthony and Jacqueline Adams. The Adams family was quintessentially British, living in Goffs Oak, a small village in Hertfordshire, not far from Harlow, Essex.

Victoria's early years were marked by a loving and supportive family. Her parents, Anthony, an electronics engineer, and Jacqueline, a former insurance clerk and hairdresser, provided the nurturing environment that would later serve as the foundation of her resilience. Their hardworking ethos and tight-knit family values left a profound imprint on young Victoria.

From a very early age, it was evident that Victoria possessed an innate passion for performing. Her parents observed her fondness for singing, dancing, and entertaining. Whether it was singing along to her favorite tunes or choreographing dances in the living room, her early creative streak was unmistakable. The living room became her stage, and the admiration of her family was her first applause.

Victoria's siblings, Louise and Christian, played crucial roles in her life. Louise, the elder sister, shared a close bond with Victoria, often indulging in dance routines together. Christian, her younger brother, was the one she protected and supported throughout their childhood. This tight sibling connection was a source of strength and support for Victoria as she journeyed toward fame.

Her parents recognized her talents and encouraged her every step of the way. Anthony and Jacqueline enrolled young Victoria in dance and modeling classes, nurturing her burgeoning skills. These early experiences were formative, providing her with the confidence and discipline that would later serve her well in the high-pressure world of show business.

The family's financial situation was not extravagant, but it was comfortable. They worked hard to provide for their children and instilled in them the values of dedication, perseverance, and humility. These qualities, more than any financial wealth, would be the driving force behind Victoria's ascent to fame and her later success as a fashion icon and businesswoman.

As Victoria's story unfolds, her childhood in Essex remains a critical chapter in the narrative. It was a time when she was just an ordinary girl with extraordinary dreams, a time when her parents' unwavering support and the simple pleasures of family life formed the bedrock upon which her future stardom would be built.

In the chapters that follow, we will journey with Victoria through the remarkable twists and turns of her life, from her days as a Spice Girl to her transformation into a global fashion icon. But let us not forget that every legend has a beginning, and for Victoria Beckham, it was in the picturesque county of Essex, amidst the embrace of family and the dreams of a young girl who would one day become an icon.

Chapter 2: Aspiring Performer

Victoria's Early Interest in Music and Dance

In the lush tapestry of Victoria Beckham's life, the threads of her destiny were woven with the silken strands of music and dance from an early age. The yearning to perform and captivate was etched into her soul long before the world knew her as Posh Spice. Chapter 2 takes us back to her formative years, unveiling the precocious talent that would one day define her as a global icon.

From the quiet streets of Goffs Oak, Essex, to the pulsating rhythm of London, Victoria's journey commenced. Born into a family of humble means, her parents, Anthony and Jacqueline Adams, recognized their daughter's affinity for music and dance. Even as a toddler, she displayed an insatiable appetite for the arts, filling the family home with the melodious echoes of her voice.

The family's influence was pivotal. Anthony, an electronics engineer, introduced Victoria to the world of technology and music, fostering her passion for the art form. Jacqueline, who had a background as an insurance clerk and hairdresser, nourished her daughter's love for dance by enrolling her in classes, an investment that would pay dividends in the years to come.

The Adams' living room was transformed into Victoria's personal stage, where she perfected her first choreographed dances and belted out her favorite songs. The cheers and applause from her family were the earliest affirmations of her extraordinary talent. It was here, within the cozy embrace of her family, that Victoria Beckham first tasted the intoxicating thrill of performing.

As she entered her formative years, Victoria's commitment to her craft intensified. Her parents recognized her gift and supported her aspirations. She began attending the Jason Theatre School in the nearby town of Cheshunt, where she honed her dancing skills and learned to shine on stage. Her relentless work ethic and dedication were already apparent, qualities that would serve her well in the high-pressure world of show business.

Victoria's journey as an aspiring performer was marked by passion and discipline. Her dance lessons, vocal training, and stage performances became her focus, and she relentlessly pursued excellence. As she grew, the recognition of her talent spread beyond the confines of her home, captivating her teachers, friends, and the local community.

It was clear to all who watched her that she had a star quality, a unique blend of charisma and talent that transcended the ordinary. While other young girls might have aspired to more typical careers, Victoria's path was set. The stage was her destiny, and the spotlight her calling.

In her teenage years, she set her sights on a career in the entertainment industry. The bustling city of London, with its rich artistic heritage, beckoned. Victoria's unwavering determination led her to audition for various roles, from modeling to acting. It was a time of intense competition, but her spirit remained unbroken.

As we traverse the pages of her life, it is crucial to understand that the journey from a small-town girl in Essex to an international icon was paved with the commitment of her family, the nurturing of her talent, and her relentless pursuit of her dreams. The humble beginnings in the suburbs would eventually give rise to a global superstar, but it was the early years of passion and dedication that set the stage for her unparalleled success.

In the chapters that follow, we will continue to unravel the layers of Victoria Beckham's extraordinary life. From her earliest days as an aspiring performer to her transformation into a Spice Girl and a fashion icon, the story of Victoria is a testament to the unwavering spirit of a girl who knew from a young age that the stage was where she belonged.

Chapter 3: Spice Girls Take the World by Storm

The Formation of the Spice Girls and Their Meteoric Rise

It was the mid-1990s, a time when the world of popular music was on the cusp of a transformation. The '90s were marked by a cultural shift, and it was within this dynamic landscape that the Spice Girls emerged. This sub-chapter takes us back to the formation of the group that would soon become a global phenomenon.

The Spice Girls were a testament to the power of collective dreams and the audacity to challenge conventions. Their story began with a serendipitous advertisement in a trade magazine, posted by Bob and Chris Herbert of Heart Management. The ad read, "R.U. 18-23 with the ability to sing/dance? R.U. streetwise, outgoing, ambitious, and dedicated?"

In response to this call to action, Victoria Adams, an aspiring performer with a burning desire for stardom, took the bold step of answering the ad. She was joined by Melanie Brown (Mel B), Melanie Chisholm (Mel C), Geri Halliwell (Ginger), and Emma Bunton (Baby). These five young women, each with their unique personalities and talents, would form the iconic quintet known as the Spice Girls.

From the outset, it was evident that the group was more than just a collection of talented individuals. They were a sisterhood, bound by a shared vision of empowerment, fun, and the celebration of girl power. Each member brought a distinct character to the ensemble. Victoria, poised and chic, embraced the persona of "Posh Spice," a moniker that would become synonymous with her name.

Their debut single, "Wannabe," released in 1996, was an instant game-changer. Its catchy melody and lyrics about the value of female friendship resonated with a generation hungry for authenticity. The accompanying music video, set in a vibrant, visually captivating mansion, captured the attention of music enthusiasts worldwide. The world was introduced to Scary, Sporty, Baby, Ginger, and, of course, Posh Spice.

The Spice Girls' meteoric rise was not just about music; it was a cultural shift. They encapsulated a sense of empowerment that transcended their catchy tunes. With their motto of "Girl Power," they struck a chord with young women everywhere, encouraging them to embrace their individuality and assert themselves. Victoria's embodiment of Posh Spice, with her sleek bob haircut and her penchant for the little black dress, became an iconic symbol of sophistication and style.

Their debut album, "Spice," was released later that year and catapulted them to international stardom. The album was an immediate chart-topper, and its impact on pop culture was undeniable. As "Wannabe" climbed the charts, the Spice Girls embarked on their whirlwind tour, captivating audiences with their exuberance and zest for life.

The Spice Girls weren't just a musical act; they were a sensation. They were a wave that washed over the world, leaving a lasting impression. In an era when the music industry was dominated by boy bands, the Spice Girls' unapologetic femininity and strength was a breath of fresh air.

Behind the scenes, Victoria was not only a performer but also a friend and confidante to her fellow Spice Girls. Their sisterhood was a powerful force, a bond that went beyond the stage. As they navigated the challenges and opportunities that came with stardom, they leaned on each other for support, creating a unique and enduring connection.

The formation of the Spice Girls marked a turning point in Victoria Beckham's life. It was a journey from the living room stage in Essex to sold-out arenas around the world. The group, with Victoria as Posh Spice, became a symbol of female empowerment, reshaping the music industry and redefining pop culture. In the chapters that follow, we will continue to trace Victoria's evolution, from her time with the Spice Girls to her subsequent transformation into a global fashion icon.

Chapter 4: The Spice Girls' Global Domination

Their Music, Style, and Impact on Pop Culture

The Spice Girls, with their undeniable charisma and girl-power anthem, weren't just a musical act. They were a cultural force, and their influence extended far beyond the boundaries of the music industry. In this chapter, we explore their global domination, highlighting the extraordinary impact they had on music, style, and pop culture as a whole.

Music was the backbone of the Spice Girls' worldwide acclaim. "Spice," their debut album, was a chart-topping phenomenon, producing hit after hit. Tracks like "Say You'll Be There," "2 Become 1," and "Stop" demonstrated their versatility and ability to resonate with a diverse audience. Each Spice Girl brought her unique vocal qualities and personality to the mix, creating a harmonious blend that struck a chord with fans worldwide.

Their lyrics weren't just catchy; they were empowering. Songs like "Wannabe" and "Spice Up Your Life" carried messages of friendship, independence, and female empowerment. The Spice Girls encouraged young women to assert themselves, be confident, and embrace their individuality. Victoria, as Posh Spice, embodied this spirit with her sophistication and style.

However, the Spice Girls' impact went beyond the realm of music. They redefined the very essence of pop culture, starting with their distinctive fashion sense. Each member represented a different archetype of style, and Victoria's Posh Spice was the epitome of chic elegance. Her signature little black dresses, sleek bob haircut, and sunglasses became iconic.

Their fashion choices were bold and unapologetic. They showed that fashion could be a form of self-expression and that there were no rules when it came to personal style. Victoria's transformation into Posh Spice introduced her to the world of fashion, a journey that would later evolve into a successful career as a fashion designer.

The Spice Girls were a pop culture revolution. They became role models for a generation of young girls, proving that they could achieve anything they set their minds to. The group's "Girl Power" mantra wasn't just a catchphrase; it was a movement that encouraged girls to dream big, be ambitious, and support one another.

Their impact on the music industry was equally profound. The Spice Girls brought girl groups back into the mainstream, paving the way for a new generation of female artists. Their influence could be seen in the success of acts like Destiny's Child, the Pussycat Dolls, and Little Mix, who followed in their footsteps.

The group's meteoric rise to global stardom was marked by sold-out concerts, merchandise frenzy, and a wave of Spice Girl-themed products. Their faces adorned magazine covers, and their music videos were celebrated for their innovative visuals. They were everywhere, from music charts to movie screens, and their influence reached all corners of the world.

Victoria's role as Posh Spice was central to the group's identity. Her elegance and sophistication resonated with fans, and her style became a fashion benchmark. The "little black dress" trend that she popularized in the '90s remains an enduring symbol of her influence on the fashion industry.

In the chapters that follow, we'll continue to delve into Victoria Beckham's remarkable journey. We'll explore her transition from a Spice Girl to a renowned fashion designer and businesswoman. Her influence on music, style, and pop culture is a testament to her enduring impact and legacy.

Chapter 5: Posh Spice Persona

Victoria's Role and Image within the Group

Within the colorful tapestry of the Spice Girls, each member played a distinct role, adding a unique hue to the group's collective identity. For Victoria Beckham, her role as Posh Spice was not just a stage persona; it became an integral part of her identity and the image of the Spice Girls as a whole.

Posh Spice was more than just a catchy nickname; it was a reflection of Victoria's poised and sophisticated demeanor. In the world of the Spice Girls, she embodied a sense of glamour and chic elegance that set her apart. Her signature style, characterized by sleek bob haircuts, designer dresses, and those iconic oversized sunglasses, became synonymous with sophistication and fashion-forwardness.

Victoria's Posh Spice persona was a testament to her ability to transform herself on stage. It wasn't just about singing and dancing; it was about portraying a character that was larger than life. In contrast to her demure demeanor offstage, when Victoria assumed the role of Posh Spice, she exuded an air of unapologetic confidence and poise.

Her image as Posh Spice became a symbol of aspiration for many young women. She showed that it was possible to be both strong and stylish, that elegance and self-assuredness could go hand in hand. In an era when the fashion world was often perceived as exclusive and unattainable, Victoria's image was relatable and inspiring.

Her role within the group extended beyond the stage. Victoria was not just a performer; she was a friend and confidante to her fellow Spice Girls. The sisterhood they formed went beyond the glitz and glamour; it was a genuine bond of support and camaraderie. This unity was a driving force behind their success, and Victoria played a pivotal role in maintaining it.

As a group, the Spice Girls were known for their empowerment anthems and messages of self-acceptance. Victoria, in her role as Posh Spice, represented a different facet of female empowerment. She demonstrated that women could be strong and elegant, sophisticated and self-assured. Her image encouraged young women to embrace their individuality and to feel confident in their style and identity.

Victoria's style choices as Posh Spice also had a lasting impact on the fashion world. The "little black dress" trend she popularized in the '90s remains a timeless symbol of her influence. Her elegance and fashion-forwardness inspired countless young women to experiment with their personal style and to see fashion as a form of self-expression.

Her journey as Posh Spice was more than just a stage act; it was a transformation that influenced her personal and professional life. It led her to explore the world of fashion and design, a passion that would later evolve into a successful career. Her ability to blend style, confidence, and elegance set her on a path to becoming a globally recognized fashion icon.

In the chapters that follow, we will continue to delve into Victoria Beckham's life and her remarkable transformation from a Spice Girl to a renowned fashion designer and businesswoman. Her role as Posh Spice was a defining chapter in her journey, shaping her image, her career, and her lasting impact on popular culture.

Chapter 6: Victoria and David Beckham

The Love Story That Captivated the World

In the annals of celebrity romances, there are few love stories that have captured the world's imagination quite like that of Victoria and David Beckham. This chapter delves into the captivating journey of their love, a union that transcended fame and left an indelible mark on the cultural landscape.

It was the late '90s when their paths first crossed, in the midst of their respective rises to stardom. Victoria Beckham, already known to the world as Posh Spice, had become an iconic figure as part of the Spice Girls. Her poised and sophisticated persona had left an impression on fans and fashion enthusiasts alike.

David Beckham, on the other hand, was on the verge of becoming a soccer superstar. As a young and talented athlete, he was making waves on the football field. It was during this moment in their lives, when their stars were ascending in their own spheres, that destiny brought them together.

Their initial meeting was set up by their respective managers, with the intention of introducing two emerging icons. As they came face to face, the chemistry was undeniable. Victoria, with her chic allure, and David, with his charisma and good looks, found themselves drawn to one another. The sparks of attraction ignited, setting the stage for a love story that would soon become the stuff of legend.

Their courtship was swift, but it was also marked by a deepening connection. They navigated the challenges of fame and the spotlight together, offering each other unwavering support. The media attention surrounding their relationship was relentless, yet it only seemed to strengthen their bond.

Their love story was punctuated by iconic moments, from the matching leather ensembles they sported early in their relationship to the engagement ring that became a symbol of their commitment. When David proposed to Victoria with a stunning diamond ring, it was a moment that made headlines and left fans swooning.

Their wedding in 1999 was a lavish affair, with a throne-like velvet-covered pew for the bride and groom. The ceremony was an epitome of celebrity extravagance, with family and friends gathered to witness their union. The world watched with bated breath as Posh Spice and the soccer icon said their vows, officially becoming Mr. and Mrs. Beckham.

Their love story, however, was not confined to grand gestures and public ceremonies. It was evident in the smaller, more intimate moments they shared, such as supporting each other's careers and raising their growing family. The Beckhams became not just a celebrity power couple, but also an example of enduring love and partnership.

As they welcomed their children—Brooklyn, Romeo, Cruz, and Harper—their family life became a testament to their commitment. They balanced their careers, parenting, and their relationship with grace and poise, showing that fame need not come at the cost of personal happiness.

The Beckhams' love story wasn't just a fairy tale; it was a testament to the strength of their bond. Through the ups and downs, the triumphs and challenges, they remained steadfast in their love and support for each other. They became an inspiration for countless fans who looked up to their enduring partnership.

In the chapters that follow, we will continue to explore the remarkable journey of Victoria Beckham. Her love story with David, marked by its passion and unwavering commitment, was just one facet of her extraordinary life. It was a union that transcended fame, captivating the world and leaving an indelible mark on the cultural landscape.

Chapter 7: Beyond the Spice: Victoria's Solo Music Career

Her Transition to a Solo Artist

As the Spice Girls' meteoric rise reached its zenith, it was inevitable that each member would explore their individual paths. For Victoria Beckham, this chapter marks the beginning of her journey as a solo artist, a transition that would test her artistic prowess and determination.

The Spice Girls had left an indelible mark on the music scene, but by the early 2000s, the group's dynamic had shifted. The girls were no longer in their 20s, and their lives were evolving. Victoria, in particular, felt the pull of her creative potential and the desire to express herself in new ways.

Her decision to step into the solo spotlight was marked by both anticipation and scrutiny. She had a reputation to uphold, both as Posh Spice and as a member of the iconic group. Victoria's solo debut came with the release of her single "Out of Your Mind" in 2000, and it was a statement of her determination to embrace her own artistic journey.

"Out of Your Mind" quickly made its way to the top of the UK charts, signaling Victoria's foray into the world of solo music. The song's catchy beat and danceable tune showcased her potential as a solo artist, while the accompanying music video demonstrated her iconic sense of style.

Her solo efforts were marked by a fusion of pop and R&B influences, exploring a sound that was distinct from the Spice Girls' catalog. Victoria, ever the perfectionist, worked diligently on her solo album. The result was "Victoria Beckham," her eponymous debut album released in 2001.

The album featured tracks like "Not Such an Innocent Girl" and "A Mind of Its Own," which were well-received by fans and critics alike. While it didn't achieve the same level of commercial success as her work with the Spice Girls, it showcased her versatility and determination as a solo artist.

Victoria's transition to a solo career was not without its challenges. The shadow of her Posh Spice persona loomed large, and the expectations were high. Yet, she was determined to forge her own path and establish her unique identity as a musician.

Her journey as a solo artist was a testament to her resilience and commitment. While she didn't reach the same stratospheric heights as she had with the Spice Girls, she had successfully rebranded herself as a solo artist with her distinct style and sound.

In the chapters that follow, we will continue to delve into Victoria Beckham's multifaceted life. Her transition to a solo artist marked a new chapter in her career, one that would lead her to explore other creative avenues and further establish her status as a global icon.

Chapter 8: Spice Girls Reunions

The Group's Reunions and Their Ongoing Legacy

As time flowed on, the allure of the Spice Girls remained intact, capturing the hearts of fans who had once danced to their tunes and fervently sang along to their anthems of girl power. The world eagerly awaited the moments when Sporty, Scary, Baby, Ginger, and, of course, Posh Spice would reunite and grace the stage once more. This chapter is a journey through the Spice Girls' reunions and the enduring legacy they've etched into the hearts of their unwavering fan base.

In 2007, after several years of individual pursuits and creative endeavors, the Spice Girls thrilled their admirers with the announcement of a long-awaited reunion tour. Titled "The Return of the Spice Girls," the tour was a sensation that crisscrossed the globe, rekindling the magic that fans had held dear for over a decade.

The news of their reunion ignited a bonfire of excitement and nostalgia that swept across the world. Those who had grown up with the Spice Girls, once carefree children dancing to "Wannabe," were now adults, but their passion for the iconic girl group hadn't waned. The anticipation was palpable, and the concerts, featuring those unmistakable melodies and signature dance moves, sold out with a speed and fervor only the Spice Girls could conjure.

The tour was not just a musical revival; it was a reaffirmation of the group's enduring power and the deep-seated impact they had on the realm of music. It also provided a new generation with the chance to witness the enchantment of the Spice Girls in the flesh. The passing years had not diminished their appeal; if anything, they had amplified it.

The fervor surrounding the reunion tour was a testament to the timeless nature of the Spice Girls' music and message. The songs that had once inspired countless young girls to embrace girl power now resonated with a diverse audience, proving that empowerment and unity are universal themes that transcend generations.

In the years that followed, there were intermittent reunions, each a spark of joy for fans who longed to see the Spice Girls united. Their performance at the closing ceremony of the 2012 London Olympics was a glorious spectacle. As they emerged from their individual pods at the center of the Olympic Stadium, clad in shimmering outfits, it was a tribute to their enduring legacy and their status as cultural icons.

These reunions weren't merely about revisiting the past; they were a manifestation of the unbreakable bond between the Spice Girls. The camaraderie and sisterhood they had fostered during their rise to stardom remained as unyielding as ever. When they took the stage, the chemistry between them was electric, and it was evident that their connection was as potent as it had been during their heyday.

As the Spice Girls continued to make sporadic appearances, their legacy continued to expand. Their influence on music and pop culture endured, and the message of girl power, which they had championed in the '90s, continued to resound with fans of all ages. Their enduring impact was a testament to the timelessness of their empowering ethos.

In the chapters that follow, we will continue to unravel the remarkable journey of Victoria Beckham. The Spice Girls' reunions were more than just a nostalgic trip down memory lane; they were a jubilant celebration of a legacy that remained as vibrant and cherished as ever. The enduring friendship between the group members and their ability to inspire and empower fans are testament to the boundless nature of girl power.

Chapter 9: Fashion Forward: Victoria's Style Evolution

Her Influence on the Fashion Industry

The evolution of Victoria Beckham, from Posh Spice to a global fashion icon, is a testament to her remarkable journey. In this chapter, we explore her style evolution and the profound influence she has had on the fashion industry, transforming herself from a pop sensation to a bona fide fashion mogul.

From the very beginnings of her career as Posh Spice, it was evident that Victoria possessed a style that set her apart. She was the epitome of chic sophistication, with her sleek bob haircut, designer dresses, and those oversized sunglasses that became iconic. But her transformation into a fashion icon went far beyond the confines of the stage.

Victoria's fashion sensibilities matured and evolved with her, leading to a journey that would eventually redefine her as a global style authority. Her personal style shifted from '90s pop diva to classic elegance, and her fashion choices reflected her evolving persona. She was no longer just a pop star; she was a trendsetter.

One of her defining moments came when she attended the Met Gala in 2008. Her choice of a dramatic, fitted gown and her now-signature pose, the "VB leg," made headlines. It was a turning point that solidified her reputation as a style icon, and the fashion world took notice.

In 2008, she launched her own eponymous fashion label, Victoria Beckham. Her debut collection received critical acclaim, establishing her as a legitimate force in the fashion industry. Her designs were characterized by their clean lines, minimalist aesthetic, and an air of understated luxury. Victoria was no longer just a wearer of fashion; she was now a creator.

As her brand gained prominence, Victoria continued to evolve her style. She embraced a modern, sophisticated look characterized by tailored blazers, wide-legged pants, and elegant silhouettes. Her attire was the embodiment of timeless chic, and it resonated with women seeking an elevated, understated sense of fashion.

Her impact on the fashion industry extended beyond her own brand. She collaborated with prestigious designers and retailers, including Marc Jacobs and Net-a-Porter. Her collection with Target in 2017 was a nod to her versatility, offering affordable fashion that maintained her signature style.

Victoria's status as a fashion authority continued to grow. Her appearances at high-profile fashion events and her participation in global fashion weeks solidified her reputation. The "VB" logo became synonymous with luxury, and her brand expanded into accessories, eyewear, and even beauty products.

Her influence on the fashion industry was undeniable. Victoria Beckham was no longer just a name associated with music and pop culture; it was synonymous with high-end, accessible luxury. She had transformed herself from a Spice Girl to a fashion powerhouse.

Her dedication to fashion extended to the business side of the industry. She embraced the challenges of entrepreneurship, navigating a male-dominated world with resilience and confidence. Her ability to create a thriving fashion brand was a testament to her business acumen.

Victoria's commitment to sustainable and ethical fashion practices was another dimension of her influence. She advocated for responsible production methods and supported initiatives that aimed to reduce the fashion industry's environmental impact. Her dedication to positive change extended beyond her own brand, demonstrating her commitment to making a difference in the industry she had come to dominate.

In the chapters that follow, we will continue to explore Victoria Beckham's multifaceted journey.

Her evolution from a pop sensation to a global fashion icon was a remarkable transformation that left an indelible mark on the fashion world. Victoria's journey was not just a personal one; it was a narrative of empowerment and redefinition, proving that one can shape their own destiny and leave an enduring legacy.

Chapter 10: Victoria Beckham: The Fashion Designer

Launching Her Eponymous Fashion Brand

Victoria Beckham's journey from Posh Spice to fashion designer extraordinaire was no small feat. This chapter takes us on her path into the world of fashion, where she transformed from a global pop icon into a respected name in haute couture, making her mark on the global fashion stage.

Her transition from the glitzy world of pop music to the hallowed halls of fashion was a deliberate and impassioned one. Victoria's deep love for fashion and her unwavering passion for design fueled this audacious leap into the industry.

In 2008, she boldly introduced her own fashion label, the Victoria Beckham brand. This wasn't a mere celebrity licensing deal; it was a fully-fledged foray into high fashion. Her debut collection was nothing short of a revelation, setting the tone for her future in the fashion world.

The designs were a reflection of her own personal style - clean, minimalist, and exuding a sense of understated luxury. It was a reflection of her modern, elegant aesthetic, and it immediately caught the eye of fashion connoisseurs and enthusiasts.

Victoria's brand rapidly ascended the ranks of high fashion. She wasn't content with merely relying on her celebrity status; she demonstrated her genuine design talent. Her creations were sought after by celebrities and fashion enthusiasts alike, solidifying her status as a legitimate force in the fashion world.

As the years progressed, her evolution as a designer was nothing short of remarkable. Her style evolved into a modern, sophisticated look that often-featured tailored blazers, wide-legged trousers, and elegant silhouettes. This was more than just clothing; it was the embodiment of timeless elegance, appealing to women in search of a refined, understated style.

Victoria's influence on the fashion world wasn't limited to what she wore or created. She extended her impact to ethical and sustainable fashion practices, advocating for responsible production methods and supporting initiatives aimed at reducing the environmental footprint of the industry. Her commitment to bringing about positive change was evident in her actions, demonstrating her power to reshape the industry for the better.

The iconic "VB" logo became synonymous with luxury, expanding into various product lines, including accessories, eyewear, and even beauty products. Her brand transcended the boundaries of fashion, encompassing a lifestyle that catered to a wide range of consumer desires.

Collaborations with esteemed designers and retailers further extended her influence, showcasing her adaptability and reach within the fashion world. The 2017 collaboration with Target exemplified her versatility, providing affordable fashion that retained her signature style.

Victoria's presence at high-profile fashion events and her participation in global fashion weeks solidified her status as a fashion authority. She consistently presented collections that enthralled the industry and spoke to a broad audience.

Her dedication extended beyond the creative aspect of fashion. She tackled the business side of the industry with resilience and confidence, all within a traditionally male-dominated arena.

In the chapters that follow, we will continue to explore the extraordinary journey of Victoria Beckham. Her transition from pop sensation to globally recognized fashion designer wasn't just a personal achievement; it was a tale of empowerment, reinvention, and the ability to shape one's destiny. Victoria Beckham, the fashion designer, had not only become a force in the industry but also an inspiration for all who dared to follow their creative passions.

Chapter 11: Building a Fashion Empire

The Success and Expansions of Her Fashion Business

Victoria Beckham's remarkable journey from Spice Girl to fashion icon reached its zenith when she ventured into the realm of fashion entrepreneurship. This chapter delves into her journey of building a fashion empire, her relentless pursuit of success, and the notable expansions that have made her brand a global force to be reckoned with.

The transition from a celebrated pop icon to a high-profile fashion designer marked Victoria's pursuit of a new passion. She was no longer content with being recognized solely as Posh Spice; her ambition extended beyond the music industry. Her desire to conquer the world of fashion was unshakable.

In 2008, Victoria launched her eponymous label, the Victoria Beckham brand. This was no celebrity vanity project; it was a full-fledged commitment to fashion. The debut collection garnered immense acclaim, establishing her as a serious contender in the world of haute couture.

Her designs embodied her personal style – elegant, modern, and infused with an understated luxury. Victoria's innate sense of aesthetics translated seamlessly into her creations, setting a standard for timeless chic that would resonate with a global audience.

As her brand ascended the echelons of high fashion, it was clear that Victoria was more than a celebrity figurehead. Her designs were celebrated by both celebrities and fashion enthusiasts, firmly establishing her reputation as a legitimate force in the fashion world. Her commitment to the craft was unwavering.

Her evolution as a designer was captivating. She embraced a modern, sophisticated look, characterized by tailored blazers, wide-legged trousers, and elegant silhouettes. Her attire wasn't just clothing; it was an embodiment of timeless elegance, catering to women who sought a refined, understated style.

But Victoria's influence wasn't confined to her own brand. She collaborated with esteemed designers and retailers, expanding her reach within the fashion world. Her 2017 collaboration with Target, for instance, showcased her adaptability and versatility, offering affordable fashion that retained her signature style.

Her presence at high-profile fashion events and her active participation in global fashion weeks cemented her status as a fashion authority. She consistently delivered collections that wowed the industry and appealed to a diverse, global audience.

The "VB" logo, synonymous with luxury, expanded into an array of product lines, including accessories, eyewear, and beauty products. Her brand had transcended the boundaries of mere fashion, transforming into a comprehensive lifestyle encompassing a wide spectrum of consumer desires.

Her influence wasn't just about what she created; it extended to ethical and sustainable fashion practices. Victoria passionately advocated for responsible production methods and supported initiatives that aimed to reduce the environmental footprint of the industry. Her dedication to effecting positive change wasn't confined to her brand but reached out to the broader fashion world, underscoring her influence as a transformative figure.

Victoria's success as a fashion designer was more than a personal achievement; it was a testament to her resilience, passion, and creative vision. She navigated the business side of the fashion industry with confidence and grace, all within a traditionally male-dominated arena.

In the chapters that follow, we will continue to unravel the remarkable journey of Victoria Beckham. Her transition from a pop sensation to a globally recognized fashion designer was not just a personal evolution; it was a narrative of empowerment, self-discovery, and redefinition. Victoria Beckham, the fashion entrepreneur, had not only become a dominating force in the industry but also an inspiration for anyone with the ambition to turn their dreams into reality.

Chapter 12: Family Life and Philanthropy

Balancing Motherhood and Her Charitable Work

While the world has recognized Victoria Beckham as a fashion icon and pop culture luminary, this chapter explores another facet of her life—her role as a dedicated mother and her commitment to philanthropic endeavors. It's a tale of balancing family life and making a meaningful impact on society.

As Victoria soared to greater heights in her fashion career, her personal life was undergoing an equally significant transformation. She was no longer just the fashion-forward icon or former Spice Girl; she was also a loving mother, dedicated to her growing family.

Victoria and her husband, David Beckham, embarked on a journey of parenthood that would bring four wonderful children into their lives: Brooklyn, Romeo, Cruz, and Harper. The couple's devotion to their children was evident, as they navigated the challenges of fame, media scrutiny, and global commitments while prioritizing their family's well-being.

Being a mother became an integral part of Victoria's identity. She embraced motherhood with grace and affection, often sharing glimpses of her family life on social media. Despite their high-profile status, the Beckhams strived to provide their children with a sense of normalcy and privacy.

Balancing her career, motherhood, and her role as a fashion mogul was no small feat, yet Victoria managed to do it with flair. Her commitment to her family was unwavering, and it was a testament to her ability to excel in multiple domains of life.

But her influence extended beyond her family. Victoria, along with her husband, engaged in various philanthropic activities. Their charitable efforts spanned a range of causes, from supporting children's hospitals to raising awareness about issues such as HIV/AIDS and malaria.

Victoria also used her fashion platform for philanthropic endeavors. She collaborated with organizations to create clothing lines where a portion of the proceeds would be directed towards charitable causes. Her commitment to giving back to the community demonstrated her desire to effect positive change in the world.

Her involvement in charitable work was marked by a genuine concern for the less fortunate and a desire to leverage her influence for the greater good. The Beckham family's dedication to philanthropy sent a powerful message about the importance of using one's platform to make a positive impact on society.

In the chapters that follow, we will continue to explore Victoria Beckham's extraordinary journey. Her life as a mother and philanthropist was not just a personal commitment; it was a narrative of love, empathy, and a dedication to making the world a better place. Victoria, the mother and philanthropist, became an inspiring figure, demonstrating that success can be measured not only by professional accomplishments but also by the positive change one brings to the lives of others.

Chapter 13: Iconic Moments and Controversies

Key Events That Shaped Her Public Image

Victoria Beckham's transition from a Spice Girl sensation to a global fashion icon was not a seamless journey. It was marked by a series of iconic moments and controversies that significantly influenced the way the world perceived her. This chapter delves into these pivotal events that shaped her public image.

One of the defining moments of Victoria's post-Spice Girls career was her bold leap into the world of high fashion. She didn't merely switch careers;

she underwent a profound transformation, redefining herself from a famous pop star to a bona fide fashion designer. Her dedication to this transition was unmistakable, and it marked a shift in her public identity.

Victoria's innate sense of style, impeccable fashion choices, and her iconic "VB leg" pose turned her into a global fashion icon. Her image graced the covers of prestigious fashion magazines, setting new standards for elegance, sophistication, and grace. The fashion world had embraced her as an authentic style authority.

However, amidst the adoration, Victoria faced her share of controversies. Her dramatic weight loss in the mid-2000s stirred public concern and ignited a broader debate about body image, the pressures within the entertainment industry, and the influence of the fashion world on societal ideals. It was a moment that prompted reflection and discussion on these critical issues.

Victoria's high-profile marriage to David Beckham became a symbol of glamour and success. Their relationship, affectionately dubbed "Posh and

Becks," was scrutinized by the media and the public. Yet, in the face of intense tabloid controversies, they emerged as an enduring power couple, serving as a symbol of resilience and unity in the midst of public scrutiny.

Her decision to reunite with the Spice Girls in 2007 was another pivotal moment in her career. The reunion tour was a celebration of the enduring bond between the group members and their ability to recreate the magic of their heyday on the stage. It was a testament to their undying camaraderie and the timelessness of their music.

However, even this iconic reunion wasn't without its share of controversies and disputes. Rumors of discord and criticisms surrounded the group, but they persevered, demonstrating their unbreakable unity and their unwavering commitment to their fans.

Victoria's dedication to philanthropy and charitable work was yet another facet of her public image. Her collaborations with charitable organizations, including those focused on HIV/AIDS and malaria, were a testament to her desire to leverage her fame for the greater good. It showcased her commitment to effecting positive change in the world, beyond the realm of fashion and entertainment.

In the chapters that follow, we will continue to peel back the layers of Victoria Beckham's multifaceted journey. Her iconic moments and controversies were not just mere incidents; they were the building blocks of a complex and inspiring narrative of triumph, resilience, and an unwavering commitment to her beliefs. Victoria, the icon, continues to inspire and captivate the world, showcasing that public perception is a multifaceted tapestry of experiences and choices.

Chapter 14: Spice Girls' Legacy

The Ongoing Impact of the Group

The Spice Girls, as a cultural phenomenon, didn't just fade into the annals of pop history. This chapter delves into the enduring legacy of the group and the lasting impact they've had on music, girl power, and the world at large.

The Spice Girls' influence on pop music transcends the boundaries of time. Their music remains iconic, with hits like "Wannabe" and "Spice Up Your Life" still resonating with audiences today. The group's ability to create catchy, empowering anthems that crossed borders and generations was nothing short of extraordinary.

But their legacy extends beyond their chart-topping songs. The Spice Girls championed "girl power," a phrase that became a global mantra for empowerment and unity among women. Their message of self-confidence, independence, and female solidarity continues to inspire women of all ages, serving as a guiding light for those who seek to shatter glass ceilings and defy societal norms.

In addition to music and empowerment, the Spice Girls' impact on pop culture was seismic. Their distinct personalities and personas became symbols of individuality and freedom. Each member represented a different facet of modern womanhood, from sporty and sexy to posh and playful. This diversity was a powerful message in itself, demonstrating that there's no single definition of "the ideal woman."

The Spice Girls' reunion tours, which delighted fans worldwide, were a testament to the timelessness of their music and the enduring connection they shared with their audience. The fervor that surrounded these reunions demonstrated that the Spice Girls' influence remained vibrant and cherished.

Even the individual pursuits of the Spice Girls have contributed to their legacy. Victoria Beckham's journey from pop star to respected fashion designer showcased the group's ability to evolve and conquer new fields while maintaining a connection to their roots.

The Spice Girls' legacy is one that continues to grow, inspiring new generations and leaving an indelible mark on the world of music, feminism, and pop culture. Their story is a testament to the enduring power of unity, empowerment, and the magic of girl power.

In the chapters that follow, we will continue to explore the multifaceted journey of Victoria Beckham. The Spice Girls' legacy is just one chapter in her remarkable life, a chapter that reflects the enduring impact of the girl group and the way it has shaped not only their careers but also their legacy.

Chapter 15: Victoria's Global Influence

Her Cultural Significance and Popularity

Victoria Beckham's influence extends far beyond her music and fashion careers. This chapter delves into her cultural significance and enduring popularity, exploring the reasons why she has become a global icon with a profound impact on society.

Victoria's journey from a Spice Girl to an internationally acclaimed fashion designer was marked by her unyielding determination and passion for her craft. Her evolution into a respected figure in the fashion world solidified her status as a cultural icon.

Her fashion sense and style choices have consistently captivated audiences around the world. She possesses a unique ability to set trends, whether it's through her iconic "VB leg" pose or her elegantly minimalist fashion designs. Her image has graced the covers of prestigious magazines, and she has been a prominent figure at global fashion events, signifying her role as a style authority.

Victoria's influence isn't confined to her fashion career alone. She's a role model for many aspiring women, showing that success can be achieved through dedication and hard work. Her journey from pop star to respected fashion designer serves as a beacon of inspiration for those who seek to break free from the limitations of their past and pursue their dreams.

Her family life with David Beckham, along with their four children, further cemented her status as a beloved and relatable figure. Her ability to balance the demands of a high-profile career with the responsibilities of motherhood resonates with many women around the world. The Beckhams' family values and dedication to their children set an example of modern family life that's both inspiring and endearing.

Victoria's commitment to philanthropy and charitable work reflects her desire to leverage her fame for the greater good. Her collaborations with charitable organizations, particularly those focused on health and children's welfare, demonstrate her genuine concern for making a positive impact on the world.

In addition to her personal endeavors, Victoria's impact extends to her contributions to the Spice Girls' enduring legacy. Their iconic music and message of "girl power" continue to inspire new generations of women. The Spice Girls remain a symbol of unity, empowerment, and diversity in a world that often struggles with these values.

Victoria Beckham's global influence is a reflection of her multifaceted journey and her ability to connect with diverse audiences. Her significance in popular culture is not solely due to her career achievements; it's also rooted in the values she represents and the inspiration she provides to people worldwide.

In the chapters that follow, we will continue to delve into Victoria Beckham's remarkable journey. Her cultural significance and popularity are not just a consequence of her fame; they are a testament to her ability to transcend boundaries and serve as a source of empowerment and inspiration for people across the globe.

Chapter 16: A Day in the Life of Victoria Beckham

Insights into Her Daily Routine and Lifestyle

Ever wondered what it's like to live a day in the life of Victoria Beckham? Here, we pull back the curtain to reveal the intricate details of her daily routine and the lifestyle that keeps her in balance, navigating seamlessly between family, career, and personal well-being.

Victoria is a firm believer in starting the day right, and that begins in the early morning hours. While most of us are still wrapped in slumber, she's already immersed in her dedication to a healthy lifestyle. Early morning workouts are non-negotiable for her. Whether it's a rigorous session with a personal trainer or a solitary Pilates practice, she kickstarts her day with exercise. It's not just about maintaining her impeccable physique; it's about feeling strong and energized, setting a positive tone for the hours ahead.

The heart of her world is her family, and her mornings often revolve around quality time with her husband, David, and their children. From a family breakfast to the school run, these moments are the anchors that keep her grounded amidst the whirlwind of her busy schedule. Her ability to balance the demands of her high-profile career with her devotion to her family is a testament to her priorities and impressive organizational skills.

The workday is a fusion of fashion design, business meetings, and creative brainstorming. As the head of her eponymous brand, her attention is indispensable. She navigates design discussions, selects fabrics, and engages in strategic business meetings. Her dedication to her brand is palpable, and her eye for detail is extraordinary.

Amid the hustle and bustle of her workday, Victoria also carves out space for wellness and self-care. During lunch breaks, you might find her meditating or indulging in a meticulously curated skincare routine. These moments of solitude provide her with a mental reset, ensuring she tackles the remainder of her day with renewed energy and unwavering focus.

The afternoons may be consumed by further meetings, fittings, or photoshoots. Victoria's meticulous approach to her work is evident in her involvement in every facet of her brand. From hand-picking materials to overseeing the final touches, her hands-on commitment mirrors her passion for her craft.

Evenings are dedicated to family moments. Whether it's preparing a hearty family dinner or attending her children's events, Victoria's evenings are an embodiment of her commitment to nurturing a loving and balanced family life. Her laughter-filled family dinners often serve as the perfect closure to a hectic day.

As the day winds down, she indulges in a relaxing skincare routine, followed by moments of quietude with her husband. The Beckhams' enduring bond is a poignant reminder of the significance of maintaining a profound connection amidst the whirlwind of their bustling lives.

Victoria's lifestyle is a testament to the power of routine and equilibrium. Her unwavering commitment to her career, her family, and her personal well-being is a testament to her extraordinary ability to manage the complexities of her multifaceted life, all while retaining a profound sense of purpose and fulfillment.

In the chapters that follow, we will continue to unveil Victoria Beckham's multifaceted journey. Her daily routine and lifestyle are testaments to her remarkable ability to sustain balance in the midst of her high-profile career and family commitments, offering insights into the practices that allow her to navigate life's intricate dance with grace and poise.

Chapter 17: Behind the Scenes: Creating Her Brand

The Work and Creativity That Fuels Her Success

In this chapter, we unveil the captivating world behind Victoria Beckham's brand, exploring the intricate work and creativity that fuel her remarkable success. From the design process to business strategies, we get a glimpse of the forces that drive her multifaceted career.

Victoria's day often commences with the earliest light, a reflection of her deep commitment to a healthy lifestyle. Her unwavering dedication to fitness leads her to early morning workouts, where the rest of the world is still in slumber. These sessions, whether led by a personal trainer or solitary Pilates practice, set the tone for her day. It's not just about maintaining her physique; it's about harnessing the energy to take on the world.

Family is at the heart of her world. Her mornings are marked by cherished moments with her husband, David, and their children. Whether it's a cozy family breakfast or the school run, these instances serve as grounding pillars amidst the whirlwind of her packed schedule. Her ability to blend her high-profile career with precious family time speaks volumes about her priorities and her remarkable organizational skills.

Victoria's workdays are an intricate dance of fashion design, business meetings, and creative brainstorming. As the head of her eponymous brand, her undivided attention is indispensable. She dives into design discussions, makes critical fabric selections, and engages in strategic business meetings. Her commitment to her brand is tangible, and her attention to detail is unmatched.

Amid the rigors of her workday, she ensures there's room for wellness and self-care. Lunch breaks become opportunities for meditation or indulging in her meticulously curated skincare regimen. These moments of solitude are her secret to a mental reset, equipping her with the energy and focus to tackle the rest of her day.

The afternoons may be consumed by additional meetings, fittings, or photoshoots. Victoria's meticulous approach to her work is apparent in her deep involvement in every facet of her brand. From choosing materials to overseeing final touches, her hands-on commitment mirrors her passion for her craft.

Evenings often revolve around family time, whether it's whipping up a hearty family dinner or attending her children's events. Her evenings are a tribute to her devotion to nurturing a loving and harmonious family life. Laughter and connection often fill her family dinners, serving as the perfect close to a bustling day.

As the day winds down, she unwinds with a relaxing skincare routine and shares moments of tranquility with her husband. The enduring bond between the Beckhams is a poignant reminder of the significance of maintaining a profound connection amidst the whirlwind of their busy lives.

Victoria's lifestyle is a testament to the power of routine and equilibrium. Her steadfast commitment to her career, her family, and her personal well-being is a testament to her extraordinary ability to navigate the intricacies of her multifaceted life while preserving a profound sense of purpose and fulfillment.

In the chapters that follow, we continue to unveil the multifaceted journey of Victoria Beckham. Her daily routine and lifestyle are glimpses into the practices that enable her to maintain balance amidst her high-profile career and family commitments, offering insights into her ability to navigate life's complex dance with grace and finesse.

Chapter 18: Victoria's Future and Enduring Legacy

What Lies Ahead and Her Place in History

As we embark on the final chapter of Victoria Beckham's remarkable journey, we are confronted with the dual mysteries of what the future holds for this iconic figure and the indelible legacy she is crafting. What lies ahead for Victoria, and where will her place be in the annals of history?

Victoria's mornings, often shrouded in the soft glow of dawn, signify her steadfast commitment to a holistic and healthy lifestyle. Her ritualistic early morning workouts, a dedicated rendezvous with a personal trainer, or a solitary engagement in the art of Pilates, serve as her daily manifesto. It is not merely about preserving her renowned physique, but about summoning the vitality to face the world.

At the core of Victoria's existence is her family, a harmonious unit composed of her beloved husband, David, and their cherished offspring. Mornings are a sacred canvas, with the strokes of family breakfasts and the canvases of school runs as her cherished masterpieces. These are not just everyday moments; they are the lifeblood of her existence, reinforcing her distinctive ability to seamlessly merge her high-profile career with these treasured family interludes.

Victoria's workdays are the conductor's wand, orchestrating the symphony of her fashion empire. As the matriarch of her eponymous brand, her role assumes a level of gravitas that is undeniable. She dabbles in design deliberations, hand-selects fabrics, and immerses herself in strategic business discussions. The commitment she pours into her brand is palpable; it is a siren song for both attention and admiration. Her fastidious eye for minutiae is unmistakable and is the hidden melody that underscores the opus of her career.

Amid the orchestration of her work, Victoria carves out interludes for moments of wellness and self-indulgence. Lunchtime intermissions metamorphose into meditative sojourns or a choreographed ballet of self-pampering through her carefully cultivated skincare ritual. These solitary moments are her secret elixirs, akin to the deep breath before an operatic aria, bestowing her with the resilience and presence needed to navigate the ensuing chapters of her day.

The afternoons unfold like an impressionist's canvas, splattered with additional meetings, fitting sessions, and photographic escapades. Victoria's tenacious tether to her work is imprinted on every facet of her brand. Whether it is the selection of materials or the meticulous examination of finishing touches, her close involvement resonates with her passion for her craft.

Evenings unfurl like a sonnet, painted with familial resonance. The suppers she lovingly concocts for her family or the performances she adoringly attends for her children become the verses of this familial symphony. These evenings are more than mere meal times or events; they are the harmonious crescendo to her daily opus.

As the nocturne of her day approaches, she embarks on a ritualistic skincare routine, cultivating a sense of closure and renewal. These twilight moments spent with her husband, the evergreen and enduring bond between the Beckhams, become the epilogue to the chapters of her day. Their connection is not just a mere footnote but a testament to the enduring love that thrives amidst the tapestry of their bustling lives.

Victoria's life is a portrayal of equilibrium and routine. Her unswerving dedication to her career, family, and personal well-being is not just a portrait but a vivid tapestry of her multifaceted existence. It is akin to an artist's brushwork, capturing the delicate balance of her life.

But as the curtain falls on this chapter, we are left pondering the unanswered questions that loom on the horizon. What does the future hold for Victoria Beckham, and how will her unique legacy be etched into the annals of history? Only time will unveil the subsequent acts of her extraordinary journey, and only the retrospective lens of history will discern the profound impact she has left on the world. Victoria Beckham's future and enduring legacy are chapters yet to be written, a riddle yet to be unraveled, and a masterpiece yet to be unveiled.

Conclusion: From Spice to Icon

Reflecting on Victoria Beckham's Remarkable Journey

As we draw the curtain on this captivating biography, it's fitting to take a moment to reflect on the extraordinary odyssey of Victoria Beckham, a journey that has carried her from the heady days of "girl power" to a status of global icon.

The story of Victoria Beckham is not just one of fame and fortune but a testament to the boundless possibilities that can be woven from sheer determination, relentless ambition, and a relentless passion for reinvention. From her beginnings as Posh Spice in the iconic girl group Spice Girls, Victoria showcased a penchant for transformation that would become the cornerstone of her life.

The dawn of her career was marked by the soaring success of the Spice Girls. Their catchy anthems and unapologetic embrace of girl power struck a chord with audiences worldwide, forging an indomitable legacy in the annals of pop music. Victoria's image as Posh Spice was emblematic of a new era in music, one where individuality and empowerment took center stage. Yet, as the Spice Girls' star ascended, so did Victoria's desire to explore new horizons.

The transition from pop sensation to revered fashion designer is a narrative rife with ambition, ambition, and an unwavering commitment to her craft. Victoria's fashion journey was not merely a career pivot but a profound transformation that demanded every ounce of her dedication. Her meticulous eye for detail, her ability to set trends, and her minimalist, sophisticated style defined a new era of fashion.

But it wasn't just in her career that Victoria left an indelible mark. Her enduring love story with David Beckham captivated the world, becoming a symbol of resilience and unity in the face of relentless media scrutiny. Their relationship wasn't just a celebrity romance; it was a testament to the enduring power of love and partnership.

Her dedication to philanthropy and charitable work reflected her desire to leverage her fame for the greater good. Her collaborations with various charitable organizations, especially those focused on health and children's welfare, demonstrated her genuine concern for making a positive impact on the world.

The Spice Girls' reunion in 2007 and their subsequent legacy tours were a celebration of the enduring bond between the group members and the timeless nature of their music. It showcased their unwavering camaraderie and the timelessness of their message.

The journey of Victoria Beckham is a testament to the multifaceted nature of a modern icon. She is a pop culture icon, a fashion maven, a loving mother, and a philanthropist. Her life, filled with the twists and turns of ambition and determination, is a story of transformation, resilience, and enduring success.

As we conclude this biography, one cannot help but wonder what the future holds for Victoria Beckham. Will she continue to reshape the world of fashion with her eponymous brand, or will new ventures beckon? Will her enduring commitment to family life remain a central theme, or will she venture into new chapters of philanthropy? These are the enigmas that the future holds, the unwritten pages of her incredible life.

What we can affirm is that the legacy of Victoria Beckham is not a mere footnote in history but a resounding chapter in the annals of contemporary culture. She has proven that an individual can transcend the confines of their past, reinvent themselves, and attain success across diverse fields. Her journey is a testament to the enduring power of ambition, the influence of individuality, and the remarkable journey from Spice to Icon. As we turn the final page, the story of Victoria Beckham continues to be written, her legacy enduring and her impact everlasting.

Printed in Great Britain
by Amazon